This book

Germ FREE Zone!!

This book is dedicated to my First Class and Year 1 best friends for always making me smile.

Printed in the United Kingdom.
First Printed 2020.

ISBN 978-1-83853-251-2

www.higermspleasegoaway.com

Hi Germs, Please Go Away!

Written and Illustrated by Channon Gray
Edited by Leah Triggs

Germs are a group of
tiny invaders
that make your
body sick and unwell.

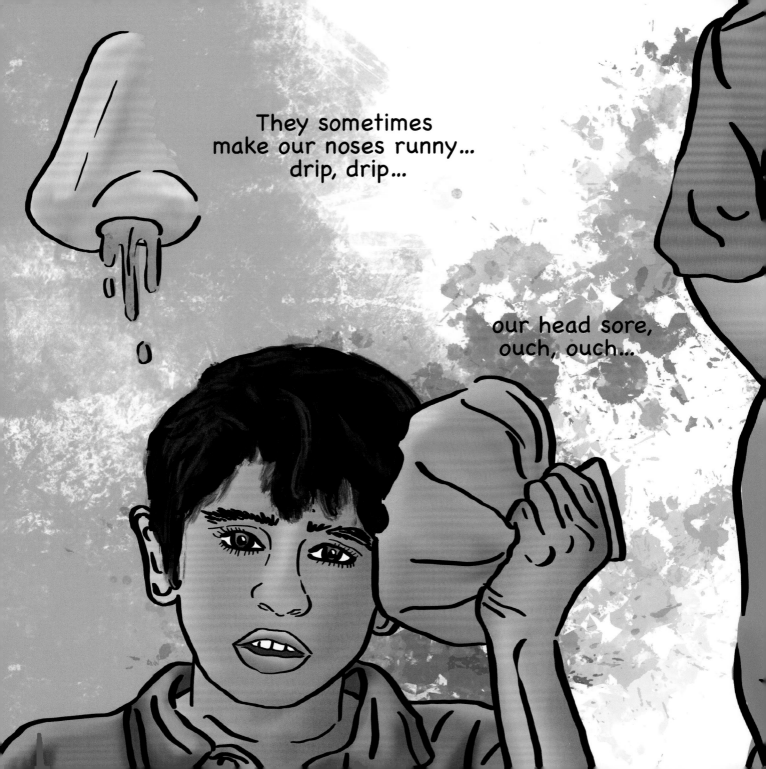

Some germs camp out in
our tummy and make it ache.
Others like to give us a sore throat
with a tickly cough and cold,
but many enjoy spreading around
to other people to make everyone
feel a bit ill.

There are **four main types of germs.**

These are...

VIRUSES, BACTERIA,

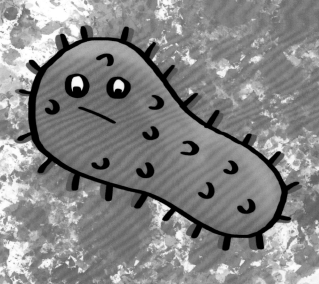

FUNGI, and PROTOZOANS.

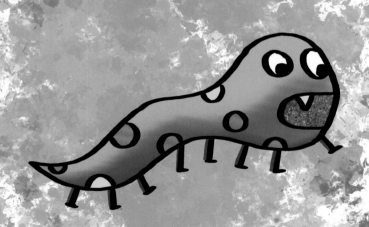

Viruses (you can say it like **vy-rus-iz**) don't survive long but cause a lot of trouble when they are alive.

Viruses live on and inside people's bodies as well as on door handles or light switches.

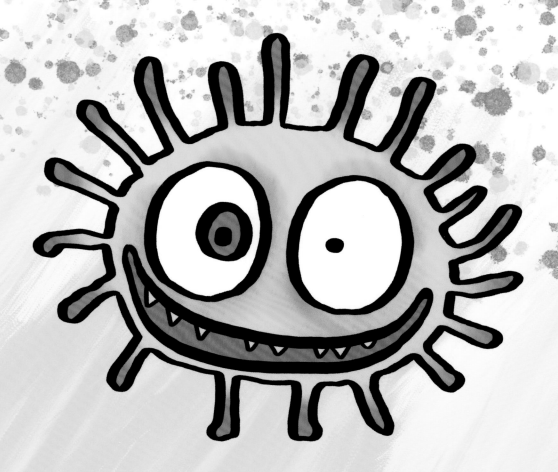

They like to spread really, **really**, **really** quickly.

You might have heard of **flu, chickenpox or measles;**
they are all viruses!

Bacteria (bak-teer-ee-uh) are like little
tiny creatures that are very small.

They can
cause nasty
infections like ear
infections,
sore throats
or cavities
in your teeth.

Some bacteria are good, and some are bad.

We have to have some good
bacteria in our bodies
to make us healthy.

It is also used to help make medicines
and vaccines that make
people better when they are poorly!

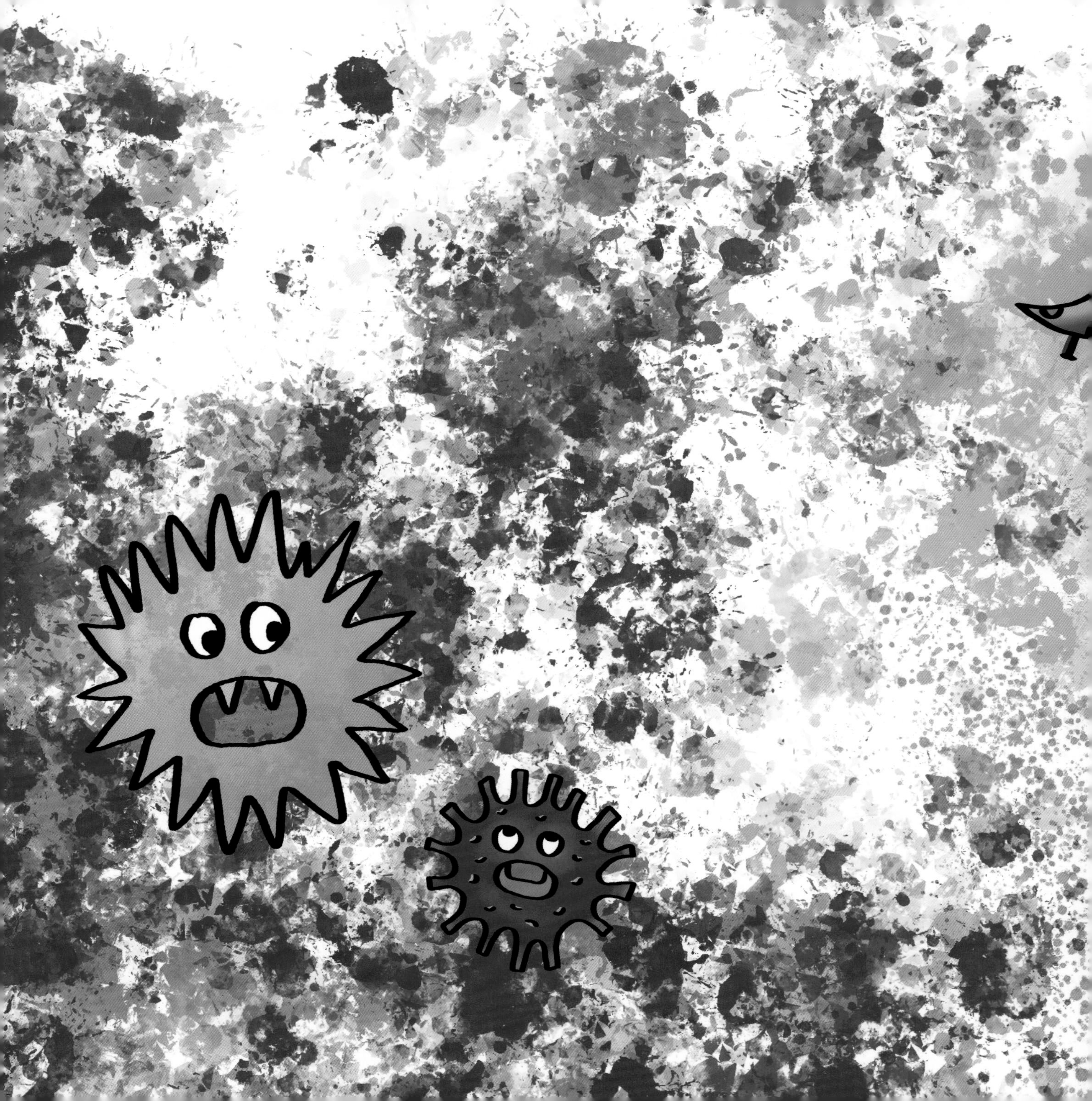

Fungi are far from fun-guys.

They like damp, warm and cosy places,
especially between people's toes.

Now, fungi can make your feet all sore
and itchy so always dry between your tiny toes.

Last of all, are the
protozoans (pro-toh-zoh-uh-ns)
now these are the germs
that make you feel sick
or have a tummy
ache.

They are **bigger** than bacteria and are known as 'parasites'.

In other words, they benefit from living on humans and other living creatures but make them sick at the same time!

Protozoans are not nice at all.

Germs like to snuggle in for a long stay.
They use up our energy supplies and can make us sick.

So, we have a message for the germs,
"Hi Germs, please go away
as it is time you found somewhere else to play!"

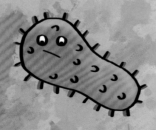

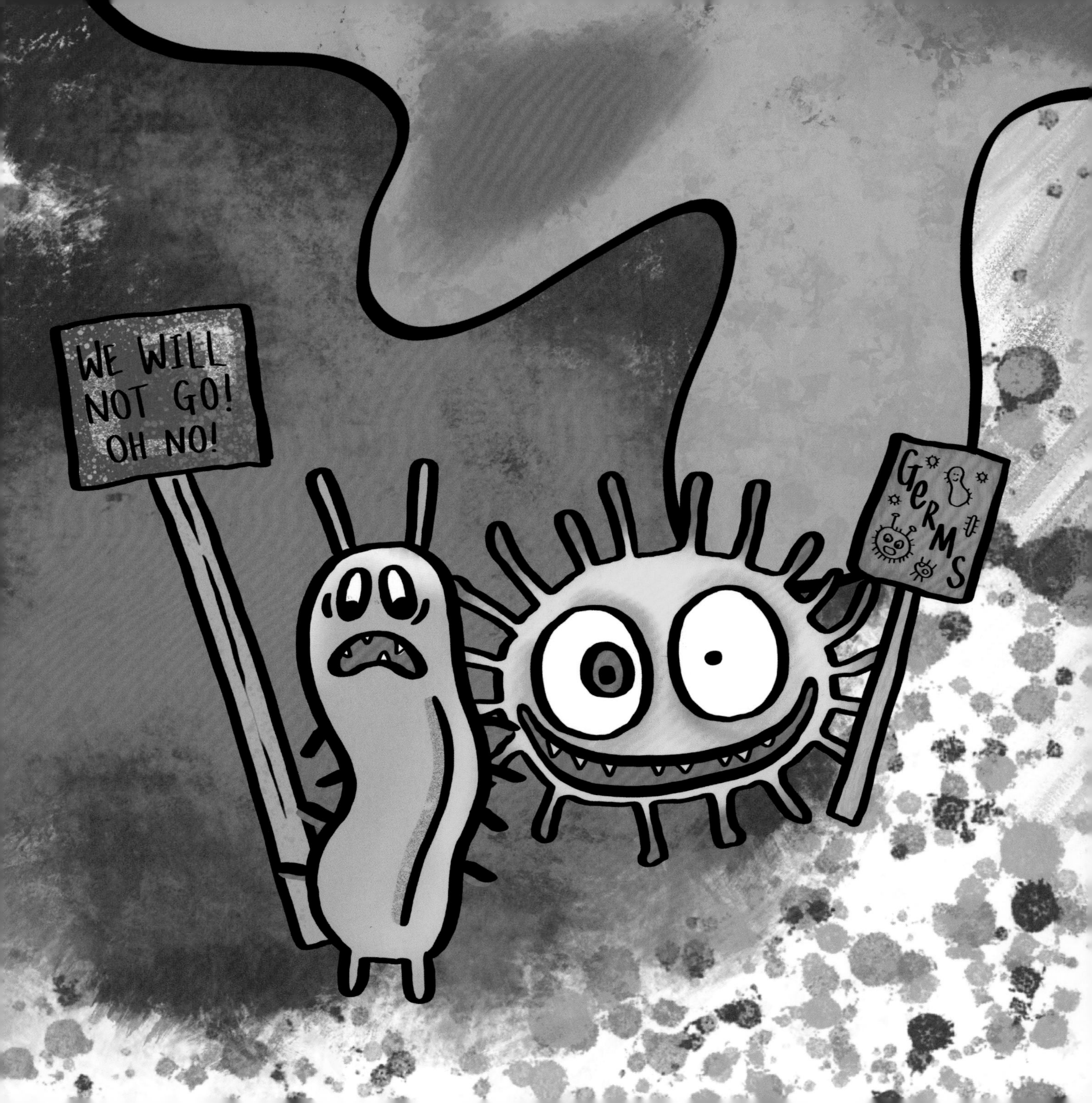
WE WILL NOT GO! OH NO!
GERMS

Germs do not like to go on their way
easily as they like to cause a fuss.

It is our job to help them
stay away from us.

We have discovered that the best way to keep all those horrible germs away is to wash your hands at least 10 times a day!

Guess what? Germs fear soap and water... it makes them rush away – hooray!

Use warm water and soap and rub your hands together for 20 seconds. Do not forget the fronts and backs, your fingertips and wrists.

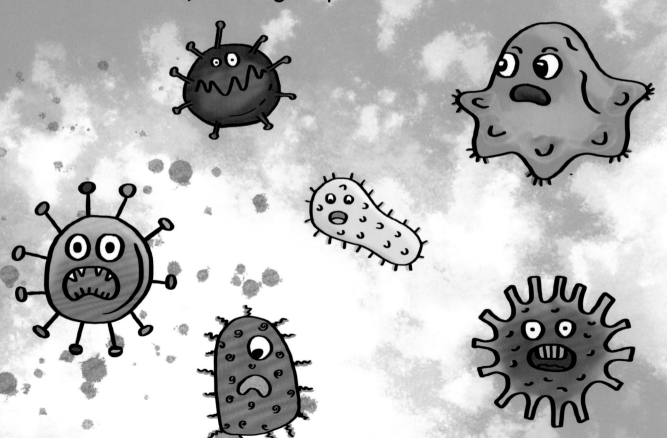

You can either sing 'Happy Birthday' two times as you scrub, or you can sing Thor's special hand-washing song to the tune of 'Baby Shark' (his favourite):

Wash your hands, doo, doo, doo, doo, doo, doo.
Wash your hands, doo, doo, doo, doo, doo, doo.
Wash your hands, doo, doo, doo, doo, doo, doo.
Wash your hands.

Goodbye germs, doo, doo, doo, doo, doo, doo.
Goodbye germs, doo, doo, doo, doo, doo, doo.
Goodbye germs, doo, doo, doo, doo, doo, doo.
Goodbye germs.

It is a good idea to catch our germs when we cough or sneeze.

It is best to cough or sneeze into your elbow to protect your hands from getting all germy (and slimy).

Then again, tissues are a super germ fighting weapon.

Just make sure
you put them straight into
the bin after you use them
(and wash your
hands again)!

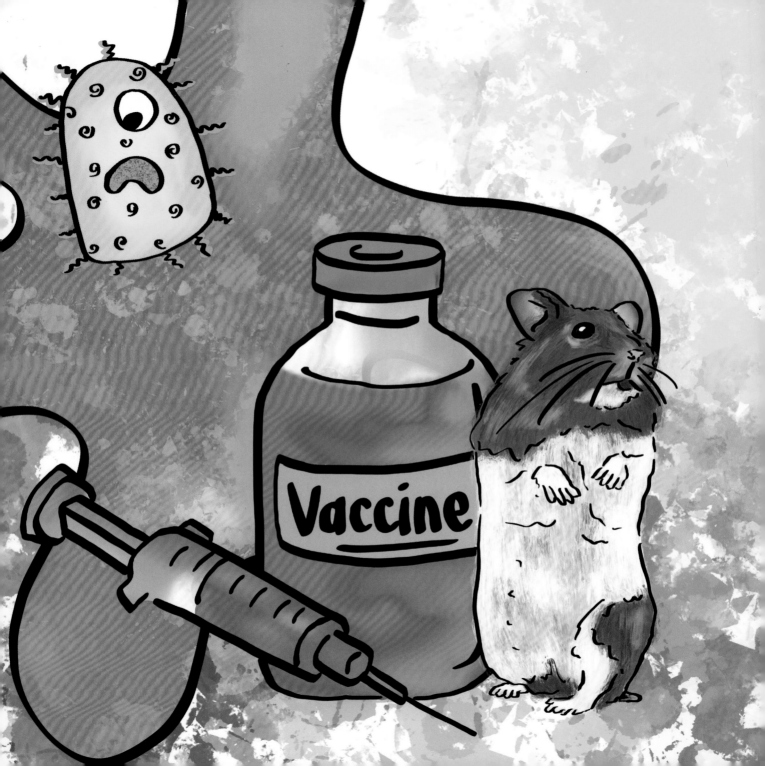

Another germ defence is getting immunisations or vaccinations to help make your body strong and able to take on battling the germs away. Lottie thinks you should ask an adult about these as us hamsters do not know much about injections these days.

You can also
keep your body safe
from germs by eating healthily,
drinking lots of water, sleeping
well and exercising.

My friends and I love
to run and run and run in
our wheels. It helps us to
get all out of puff.

We think that you are now ready to take on the germs.
What do you think?

For more, please visit:
www.higermspleasegoaway.com

About the Author (and Hamsters)

Channon is a Primary School Teacher from Cornwall.
She likes drawing, walking along the beach, talking to her
cats and eating ice-cream on a stormy day.

She has four pet hamsters: Bear, Oreo, Lottie and Thor. They
are Syrian Hamsters and their favourite treats are
monkey nuts, hammy chocolate drops and sunflower seeds - yum!

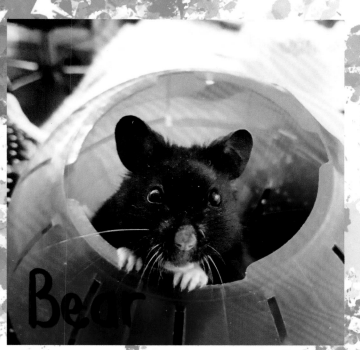

Bear

Thor

Oreo

Lottie